Certificate III in Business
Apply critical thinking skills in a team environment
Core topic workbook

Linda Joel

A
FIVE SENSES
PUBLICATION

Five Senses Education Pty Ltd
2/195 Prospect Highway
Seven Hills 2147
New South Wales
Australia

© Five Senses Education Pty Ltd and Linda Joel
First Published 2022

Joel, Linda
Certificate III in Business
Apply critical thinking skills in a team environment
Core topic workbook

ISBN 978-1-76032-498-8

Contents

A glossary of key words for assessment

Using the glossary will help students to understand what is expected in responses in examinations and assessment tasks.

Account: Account for: state reasons for, report on. Give an account of: narrate a series of events or transactions

Analyse: Identify components and the relationship between them; draw out and relate implications

Apply: Use, utilise, employ in a particular situation

Appreciate;   Make a judgement about the value of

Assess: Make a judgement of value, quality, outcomes, results or size

Calculate: Ascertain/determine from given facts, figures or information

Clarify: Make clear or plain

Classify: Arrange or include in classes/categories

Compare: Show how things are similar or different

Construct: Make; build; put together items or arguments

Contrast: Show how things are different or opposite

Critically: Add a degree or level of accuracy depth, knowledge and understanding,

(analyse/ evaluate)   logic, questioning, reflection and quality to (analyse/evaluate)

Deduce: Draw conclusions

Define: State meaning and identify essential qualities

Demonstrate: Show by example

Describe: Provide characteristics and features

Discuss: Identify issues and provide points for and/or against

Distinguish: Recognise or note/indicate as being distinct or different from; to note differences between

Evaluate: Make a judgement based on criteria; determine the value of

Examine: Inquire into

Explain: Relate cause and effect; make the relationships between things evident; provide why and/or how

Extract: Choose relevant and/or appropriate details

Extrapolate: Infer from what is known

Identify: Recognise and name

Interpret: Draw meaning from

Investigate: Plan, inquire into and draw conclusions about

Justify: Support an argument or conclusion

Outline: Sketch in general terms; indicate the main features of

Predict: Suggest what may happen based on available information

Propose: Put forward (for example a point of view, idea, argument, suggestion) for consideration or action

Recall: Present remembered ideas, facts or experiences

Recommend: Provide reasons in favour

Recount: Retell a series of events

Summarise: Express, concisely, the relevant details

Synthesise: Putting together various elements to make a whole

Chapter 1: Prepare to address workplace problem

Short answers:

1. What is involved in brainstorming possible solutions to a problem?   (2 marks)

    _____

    _____

    _____

    _____

2. How can you monitor and evaluate a solution to a problem?   (2 marks)

    _____

    _____

    _____

    _____

3. What does poor work-life balance mean?   (2 marks)

    _____

    _____

    _____

    _____

4. Identify four other common problems encountered by workers.   (4 marks)

    _____

    _____

    _____

    _____

5. Identify four common problems encountered by businesses and explain why they are a problem.   (4 marks)

    _____

    _____

    _____

    _____

    _____

    _____

_____

_____

_____

6. What is team cohesion? (2 marks)

_____

_____

_____

7. How does bullying and harassment impact a workplace? (2 marks)

_____

_____

8. What is the difference between overt and covert bullying? (2 marks)

_____

_____

9. Identify and describe the main types of bullying and harassment. (8 marks)

_____

_____

_____

_____

_____

_____

_____

_____

_____

_____

_____

_____

_____

_____

_____

10. What effects can bullying and harassment have on the person being bullied?   (3 marks)

_____

_____

_____

_____

_____

11. What constitutes a safe working environment for workers?   (2 marks)

_____

_____

_____

12. What type of behaviour would be deemed as bullying or harassment?   (2 marks)

_____

_____

_____

13. What is the difference between bullying, conflict and teasing?   (3 marks)

_____

_____

_____

_____

14. Other than the person being bullied, who else can be affected by this type of behaviour?

(2 marks)

_____

_____

_____

15. If being bullied, why is it important to keep a diary of what has happened?   (2 marks)

_____

_____

_____

16. What data could indicate to a PCBU that bullying and harassment could be occurring?

(3 marks)

_____

_____

_____

Multiple choice:

1. When trying to solve a problem, what comes under the heading "define the problem"?
    a. Consult with others
    b. What and where it is
    c. Separate fact from fiction
    d. Look at positives and negatives

2. When do workers feel undervalued?
    a. When work schedules are inflexible
    b. When communication is only one way
    c. When there is little opportunity for promotion
    d. When inadequate facilities are provided for workers

3. What is a common problem encountered by businesses?
    a. Uncertainty of the future
    b. Lack of accountability of workers
    c. Lack of suitable training for workers
    d. Ineffective job performance reviews

4. What is considered to be overt bullying or harassment?
    a. Negatively influencing projects
    b. Taking credit for other people's work
    c. Belittling another worker in meetings
    d. Excluding someone from a conversation

5. What is an example of psychological bullying or harassment?
    a. Telling someone they are dumb
    b. Making sexually explicit comments
    c. Playing mind games with fellow workers
    d. Continually slapping someone on the head

6. What can be the result of continual bullying and harassment?
    a. The victim can gain or lose weight
    b. The perpetrator changes jobs more often
    c. The victim becomes more popular at work
    d. The perpetrator's behaviour changes over time

7. What is the AHRC?
    a. Australian Human Rights Commission
    b. Australasian Human Rights Commission
    c. Australian Humanitarian Rights Commission
    d. Australasian Humanitarian Rights Commission

8. What skill should a person being bullied be taught?
    a. Acceptance
    b. Assertiveness
    c. Empathy
    d. Responsibility

9. Who are the key stakeholders in cases of bullying and harassment?
    a. Visitors, victim, families, business owner
    b. Victim, families, witnesses, business owner
    c. PCBU, business manager, victim, witnesses
    d. Aggressor, victim, witnesses, business owner

10. Who should be asked the question "would you like to be treated in the same way?"
    a. Family
    b. Witness
    c. Aggressor
    d. Business owner

11. What question should the PCBU be asked about bullying and harassment?
    a. Have you reported it?
    b. Are you treating every worker fairly?
    c. What effect does it have on witnesses?
    d. Do you promote a positive work environment?

True or false?

12. Problem-solving is an important skill that workers need these days.

13. Most workplace problems are straightforward and easy to fix.

14. Choosing the best course of action to solve a problem often creates more problems.

15. When monitoring a situation, changes are made as needed.

16. Poor leadership helps improve the motivation of workers.

17. The higher up the management level, the more problems will be encountered.

18. Two-way communication between supervisors and workers rarely happens.

19. Lack of suitable training results in mistakes being made and management being pleased with worker performance.

20. A common problem encountered by businesses is decreased competition.

21. It is important for businesses to keep up with technological change.

22. Bullying and harassment causes psychological harm.

23. Even work experience students can be subjected to bullying and harassment.

24. Some types of workplace bullying are criminal offences.

25. Covert bullying and harassment is obvious.

26. Constant teasing or playing practical jokes on someone is considered to be overt.

27. Setting tasks that are either well below or above someone's level of skill is considered to be overt.

28. Physical bullying includes tripping, shoving and grabbing.

29. Sexual bullying and harassment includes sending suggestive emails or texts.

30. Bullying and harassment usually occurs spasmodically.

31. A Dignity and Respect in the Workplace Charter and assist workers to understand their rights and responsibilities.

32. A commitment to diversity recognises differences among all workers.

33. Harassment is occurring if behaviour is reasonable and welcomed.

34. A letter of apology from the victim of bullying and harassment is a positive outcome.

35. Bullying and harassment is based on a power imbalance.

36. Bullying and harassment should first be reported to a supervisor.

37. Bullying and harassment is uncommon but normal.

38. The PCBU has the duty of care for the health and wellbeing all of workers while at work.

39. Witnesses of bullying and harassment should intervene to stop it.

40. Bullying and harassment results in lower absentee rates and higher turnover of workers.

Write clues for the following completed crossword:

Across:

2. _____

_____

6. _____

_____

7. _____

_____

8. _____

_____

10. _____

_____

13. _____

_____

14. _____

_____

16. _____

_____

17. _____

_____

19. _____

_____

Down:

1. _____

_____

3. _____

_____

4. _____

_____

5. _____

_____

9. _____

_____

11. _____

_____

12. _____

_____

15. _____

_____

16. _____

_____

18. _____

_____

Answer the following crossword:

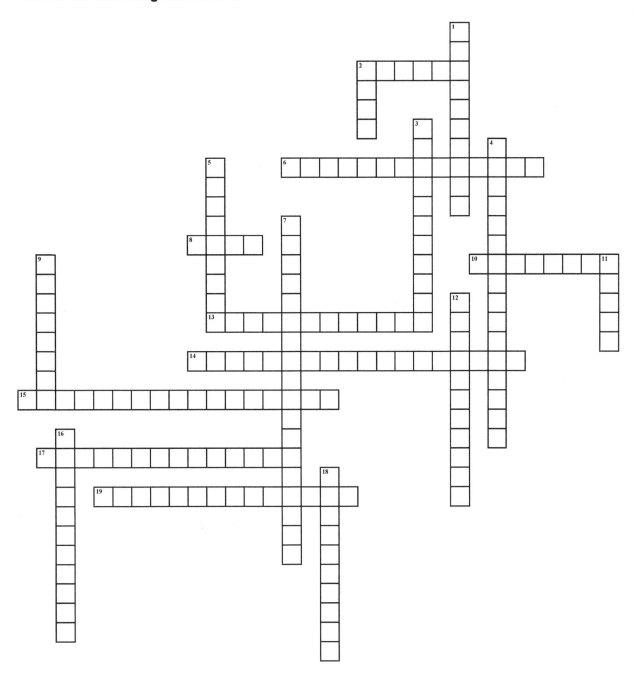

Across:

2. This form of bullying often involves unwelcome touching.

6. This usually decreases due to the lack of training.

8. This increases for the victim with increased frequency of bullying and harassment.

10. Frequency of unwanted behaviour.

13. These include the victim, the aggressor, witnesses and the PCBU.

14. Setting an unreasonable timeline to complete work in, is an example of this. (2 words)

15. This is part of the implementation of a solution to curb a problem. (2 words)

17. The overall effect of bullying and harassment. (2 words)

19. This must be easy to implement and be acceptable to everyone if a problem is to be solved. (3 words)

Down:

1. Verbal insults are this.

2. This type of work environment should be provided by the PCBU.

3. These people should always work well together and support each other. (2 words)

4. Conflict is often the result of this.

5. These people should intervene to stop bullying and harassment from occurring.

7. This can suffer if bullying and harassment affects worker productivity and quality of output. (2 words)

9. The manner in which teams should work.

11. This should be kept by victims of bullying and harassment.

12. This can occur for an aggressor if they do not change their behaviour.

16. These often change which can cause many problems for a business.

18. The PCBU can look at these to gather supporting evidence that a problem exists.

Extended response 1:

a) Explain the types of problems that can occur in the workplace. (3 marks)

_____

_____

_____

_____

_____

_____

b) Identify the steps that should be taken to solve a problem in the workplace. (3 marks)

_____

_____

_____

_____

_____

_____

_____

_____

_____

_____

_____

_____

_____

c) Explain the different types of bullying and harassment and how they can affect the person being bullied or harassed. (9 marks)

_____

_____

_____

_____

_____

_____

_____

_____

_____

Apply critical thinking skills in a team environment   © Five Senses Education Pty Ltd and Linda Joel

Extended response 2:

Describe a Dignity and Respect in the Workplace Charter. Explain the reasons for implementing this type of policy and procedures.   (15 marks)

Your answer will be assessed on how well you:
- demonstrate knowledge and understanding relevant to the question
- communicate ideas and information using relevant workplace examples and industry terminology
- present a logical and cohesive response

_____

_____

_____

_____

_____

_____

_____

_____

_____

_____

_____

_____

_____

_____

_____

_____

_____

_____

_____

_____

_____

_____

_____

_____

Apply critical thinking skills in a team environment

Chapter 2: Evaluate solutions for workplace problem

Short answers:

1. Define critical thinking. (2 marks)

_____

_____

_____

2. Identify the skills used in critical thinking. (4 marks)

_____

_____

_____

_____

_____

3. Define risk assessment. (2 marks)

_____

_____

4. What is a risk assessment matrix? (2 marks)

_____

_____

_____

5. What guidelines should be included in a bullying and harassment policy and procedures?

(2 marks)

_____

_____

6. What is awareness raising, with respect to bullying and harassment? (2 marks)

_____

_____

_____

_____

7. What is leadership training, with respect to bullying and harassment? (2 marks)

_____

_____

_____

8. Identify the changes that could be made at the job level to minimise bullying and harassment. (3 marks)

_____

_____

_____

_____

9. Define mediation. (2 marks)

_____

_____

_____

10. Outline the steps taken when developing a new policy. (3 marks)

_____

_____

_____

_____

_____

11. Define criteria. (2 marks)

_____

_____

_____

12. How does training of workers reduce the risk of bullying and harassment occurring in the workplace? (2 marks)

_____

_____

_____

Multiple choice:

1. What does critical thinking allow you to do?
    a. Ask a lot of questions
    b. Look at things without bias
    c. Make logical and informed decisions
    d. Assume nothing without asking questions

2. How should you determine relevance?
    a. By making an educated guess
    b. By not taking anything for granted
    c. Seeing if the language distorts the facts
    d. Looking at information with a clear objective

3. What is the risk of something happening if the probability is low and the severity can be very harmful?
    a. None
    b. Low
    c. Medium
    d. High

4. When developing strategies to stop bullying and harassment in the workplace, what is the first step in the risk assessment process?
    a. Assessing the risk of potential harm to workers
    b. Considering if workers are at risk of bullying and harassment
    c. Assessing what risks can or can't be controlled in the workplace
    d. Raising awareness of bullying and harassment to see if it stops first

5. Why would a new policy be most successful when implemented?
    a. If it is included in the policies and procedures manual
    b. If it clarifies what is appropriate and inappropriate behaviour at work
    c. If it is created by representatives of both management and workers
    d. If the leaders are fully trained to raise the awareness of the new policy

6. How can the culture change to lessen the incidents of bullying and harassment?
    a. By introducing team bonding sessions
    b. By changing the work hours of all workers
    c. By changing the physical work environment
    d. By introducing more training and development sessions

7. What is often included in worker education to reduce bullying and harassment?
    a. Simulated mediation sessions
    b. Worker responsibilities when witnessing bullying
    c. Coaching sessions so workers know the correct way to bully someone
    d. An integrative approach about how to bully and what to do when bullied

8. How much bullying and harassment should be tolerated in the workplace?
   a. Zero
   b. One incident a week
   c. Two incidents a week
   d. Three or more incidents a week

9. Who has the greatest influence when creating a positive work environment?
   a. Management
   b. Supervisors
   c. Team members
   d. Workers

10. What is the most important when developing a new policy?
    a. Drafting the policy
    b. Determining the content
    c. Setting an implementation date
    d. Communicating it to all stakeholders

11. What Act requires works to be trained about bullying and harassment in the workplace?
    a. Fair Work Act
    b. Anti-Discrimination Act
    c. Sex Discrimination Act
    d. Work Health and Safety Act

12. What is an advantage of awareness raising regarding bullying and harassment?
    a. Actions that can be taken are outlined
    b. Provides clear and consistent responses
    c. Covers best practice for dealing with problems
    d. Any tensions between workers can be reduced

13. What is a disadvantage of changing working conditions to reduce bullying and harassment?
    a. Not as many workers may be as happy
    b. Changes may work for a very short period of time
    c. Some workers could get better conditions than others
    d. The victim and aggressor may end up working in the same area

14. What is a purpose of holding coaching sessions about bulling and harassment?
    a. To prepare workers for what may happen in real time
    b. To show workers what constitutes bullying and harassment
    c. So workers have a prepared plan if they are bullied or harassed
    d. So workers are taught how inappropriate behaviour affects people

15. What is an advantage of mediation in cases of continued bullying and harassment?
    a.   It isn't compulsory
    b.   The process is quick
    c.   A result is always guaranteed
    d.   Any party can withdraw at any time

True or false?

16. Information from an unverified source could raise a red flag.

17. A question that could be asked when identifying a problem is: Who benefits?

18. Inference is the ability to draw conclusions.

19. Deciding if information is relevant is easy.

20. Always ask open and closed questions to satisfy curiosity.

21. People with critical thinking skills can identify inconsistencies and errors.

22. Risk assessment measures the likelihood and severity of injury occurring.

23. A risk assessment matrix is an important part of the risk assessment process.

24. A risk assessment matrix goes from very low to very high risk.

25. Solutions to bullying and harassment can be implemented at the business level, the job level and at the worker level.

26. The last step in a risk assessment process is implementing the controls.

27. An anti-bullying and harassment policy is often referred to as a Dignity and Respect in the Workplace Policy.

28. Leadership training enables workers, supervisors, leaders and managers to understand the fundamentals of bullying and harassment.

29. At the job level, there should be a focus on minimising the occurrence of bullying and harassment.

30. Working conditions includes demands placed on workers, training, work hours, and health and wellbeing standards.

31. Workplaces that are hot, noisy, cramped or do not have enough equipment for individual workers have a lot of room for improvement as these conditions can lead to more bullying and harassment.

32. Staggering lunch times could separate those being bullied from their aggressor.

33. Training should be provided for those bullying others about what is considered to be appropriate behaviour in the workplace.

34. Cognitive rehearsal teaches workers to have a prepared plan to respond respectfully when being bullied or harassed.

35. Mediation involves a worker from another department as an independent and impartial third party who facilitates open discussions between the worker being bullied, harassed and the perpetrator.

36. An integrative approach uses one strategy to comprehensively address bullying and prevent its recurrence.

37. All workers contribute to the workplace culture which sets the standards and behaviours that exist in each workplace.

38. Training doesn't reduce the risk of bullying and harassment occurring because it builds worker confidence in the business's anti-bullying and harassment policy.

39. The type of training regarding bullying and harassment will usually depend on the needs identified through the risk assessment process.

40. Workplace policies will cover all types of bullying and harassment that could occur in the workplace.

41. Team bonding sessions always relieve tensions between workers.

42. It is expensive to implement some changes in the workplace to reduce bullying.

43. Any prepared plans covered in cognitive rehearsal may be forgotten when being bullied.

44. No single strategy or initiative should be used on its own to prevent and manage bullying and harassment.

45. Punitive action for those found to be bullying or harassing others must be applied immediately to reduce inappropriate behaviour.

Write clues for the following completed crossword:

Across:

3. _____

_____

7. _____

_____

9. _____

_____

11. _____

_____

13. _____

_____

15. _____

_____

17. _____

_____

18. _____

_____

19. _____

_____

20. _____

_____

Down:

1. _____

_____

2. _____

_____

4. _____

_____

5. _____

_____

6. _____

_____

8. _____

_____

10. _____

_____

12. _____

_____

14. _____

_____

16. _____

_____

Answer the following crossword:

Across:

3. The ability to make an educated guess.

4. This must be done to all data collected to determine if it is reliable.

8. This is done after any risks are identified. (2 words)

10. Principles or standards by which something may be judged or decided.

11. Critical thinking skills can be used to identify these.

16. Without this, any new policy may not be successful.

17. Type of behaviour that should be stamped out in the workplace.

18. Probability of bullying and harassment occurring.

19. When decisions are based on intelligent thinking.

20. These can hinder the process of critical thinking. (2 words)

Down:

1. This is needed if data collected is to be believed.

2. Workers are taught about these in cognitive rehearsal sessions. (2 words)

5. These people have the responsibility in creating a workplace free from bullying.

6. This approach effectively addresses bullying and harassment. (2 words)

7. Using simulation exercises to prepare workers for what may happen in real time. (2 words)

9. This should be done on a regular basis.

12. These are part of working conditions. (2 words)

13. Each one of these must be evaluated for flaws.

14. How often should policies and procedures be reviewed?

15. These people can also be affected by the bullying and harassment of workmates.

Extended response 1:

a) What role does worker education have in reducing bullying and harassment in the workplace? (3 marks)

_____

_____

_____

_____

_____

_____

b) Explain the steps taken in the risk assessment of bullying and harassment. (4 marks)

_____

_____

_____

_____

_____

_____

_____

_____

_____

_____

_____

_____

_____

c) Evaluate possible strategies that can be taken to eliminate bullying and harassment in the workplace. (8 marks)

_____

_____

_____

_____

_____

_____

_____

Apply critical thinking skills in a team environment

Extended response 2:

Explain how critical thinking skills can generate solutions to the problem of bullying and harassment in the workplace. (15 marks)

Your answer will be assessed on how well you:
- demonstrate knowledge and understanding relevant to the question
- communicate ideas and information using relevant workplace examples and industry terminology
- present a logical and cohesive response

_____

_____

_____

_____

_____

_____

_____

_____

_____

_____

_____

_____

_____

_____

_____

_____

_____

_____

_____

_____

_____

_____

_____

Apply critical thinking skills in a team environment   © Five Senses Education Pty Ltd and Linda Joel

Chapter 3: Finalise and review solution development process

Short answers:

1. What is an anti-bullying and harassment policy often referred to as? (1 mark)

_____

2. What steps are involved when determining the content for a new policy? (2 marks)

_____

_____

_____

3. Why is a policy regarded as a living document? (2 marks)

_____

_____

4. How accessible should be an anti-bullying and harassment policy? (2 marks)

_____

_____

_____

_____

5. What is natural justice in a bullying or harassment case? (2 marks)

_____

_____

_____

_____

6. What does the successful performance in business require? (2 marks)

_____

_____

_____

_____

7. What is the difference between intuitive and reflective critical thinking processes? (4 marks)

_____

_____

_____

_____

_____

_____

_____

_____

8. What is the purpose of asking questions during the critical thinking process? (2 marks)

_____

_____

_____

9. Identify the eight elements of thinking. (8 marks)

_____

_____

_____

_____

_____

_____

_____

_____

10. Why should problems be solved by more than one person rather than by just one individual worker? (2 marks)

_____

_____

_____

_____

Multiple choice:

1. When do you ask questions like who, what and why?
   a. When revising an old policy
   b. When identifying the need for a new policy
   c. When conducting research into a new policy
   d. When determining the content of a new policy

2. To whom should a draft copy of a new bullying and harassment policy to given to for feedback?
   a. Stakeholders
   b. Management
   c. Owner of the business
   d. Victims of bullying and/or harassment

3. Where should an anti-bullying and harassment policy be stored?
   a. On the internet
   b. On the intranet
   c. On the owner's computer
   d. In the owner's personal filing cabinet

4. Who should be given information about a bullying complaint?
   a. The police
   b. All the workers
   c. Only those who need to know
   d. Just the aggressor and the victim

5. All complaints must be dealt with fairly, promptly and efficiently. What is this known as?
   a. Accessibility
   b. Confidentiality
   c. Natural justice
   d. Procedural fairness

6. What type of critical thinking process makes judgements based on reasoning?
   a. Intuitive
   b. Procedural
   c. Reactive
   d. Reflective

7. What question could be asked during the inference stage of critical thinking?
   a. Do we need more information?
   b. What conclusions can be drawn?
   c. How was the analysis conducted?
   d. Are we confident in the conclusions?

8. What are consequences?
   a. Assumptions
   b. Implications
   c. Perspectives
   d. References

True or false?

9. The best solution to end bullying and harassment in the workplace is to develop an anti-bullying and harassment policy,

10. An anti-bullying and harassment policy is often referred to as a Dignity and Respect in the Workplace Charter.

11. Once a new policy has been distributed, there is no need for consultation and feedback.

12. To analyse information means to draft a new policy.

13. An anti-bullying and harassment policy must be virtually published.

14. A living document is one that grows on trees.

15. Communication is the key for a policy to be successful.

16. All bullying and harassment should be reported immediately.

17. An anti-bullying and harassment policy should only be written in English.

18. All policies should be written in straightforward language with the use of acronyms so everyone can understand them.

19. Natural justice occurs when both parties have the right to be heard.

20. If an allegation of bullying or harassment is proven, action taken will depend on the seriousness of the situation.

21. Victims of bullying and harassment usually have their employment terminated.

22. If there are threats of violence, the Police can be called.

23. Incidents of bullying can be reported to SafeWork NSW on 000.

24. Strength in critical thinking results in business success.

25. Teams must work together to work through problematic situations in order to arrive at reasonable conclusions.

26. Critical thinking is an individual process.

27. Evaluation looks at the validity of the conclusions.

28. Not much of our thinking is biased.

29. Purposes of thinking includes goals and issues.

30. Thinking usually embodies a point of view or perspective.

31. If inferences change, you have to change your assumptions.

32. If the assumptions change, the questions asked will be different.

33. Thinking is defined by ten elements.

34. Some problems can be handled by one person while others depend on a team approach to solve them.

35. Bullying and harassment usually occurs on an individual level but the implications can affect a whole team and their productivity.

Write clues for the following completed crossword:

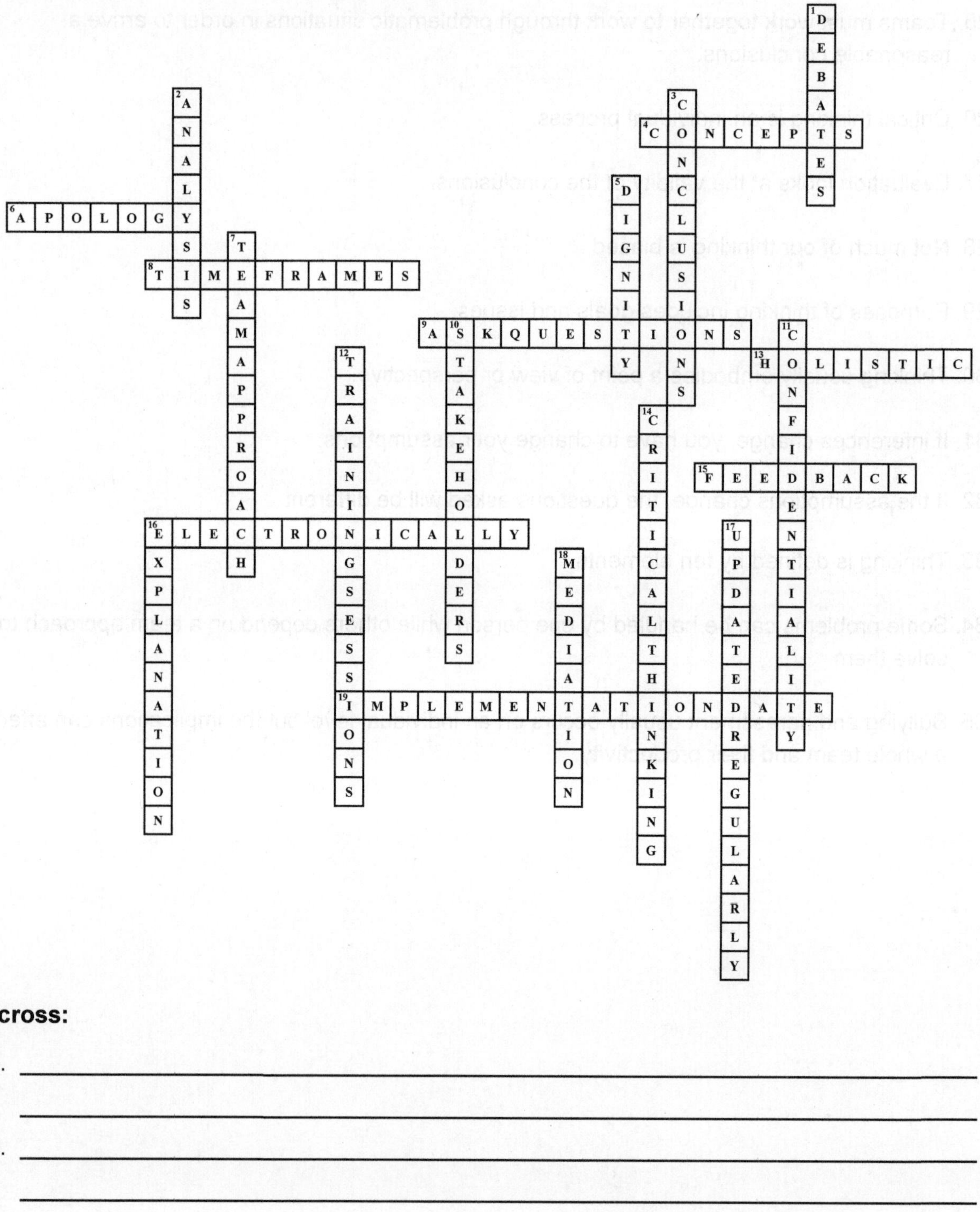

1 DEBATES
2 ANALYSIS
3 CONCLUSIONS
4 CONCEPTS
5 DIGNITY
6 APOLOGY
7 TEAMAPPROACH
8 TIMEFRAMES
9 ASKQUESTIONS
10 STAKEHOLDERS
11 CONFIDENTIALITY
12 TRAININGSESSIONS
13 HOLISTIC
14 CRITICALTHINKING
15 FEEDBACK
16 ELECTRONICALLY
16 EXPLANATION
17 UPDATEDREGULARLY
18 MEDIATION
19 IMPLEMENTATIONDATE

Across:

4. ______________________________

____

6. ______________________________

____

8. ______________________________

____

9. ______________________________

____

13. _____

_____

15. _____

_____

16. _____

_____

19. _____

_____

Down:

1. _____

_____

2. _____

_____

3. _____

_____

5. _____

_____

7. _____

_____

10. _____

_____

11. _____

_____

12. _____

_____

14. _____

_____

16. _____

_____

17. _____

_____

18. _____

_____

Answer the following crossword:

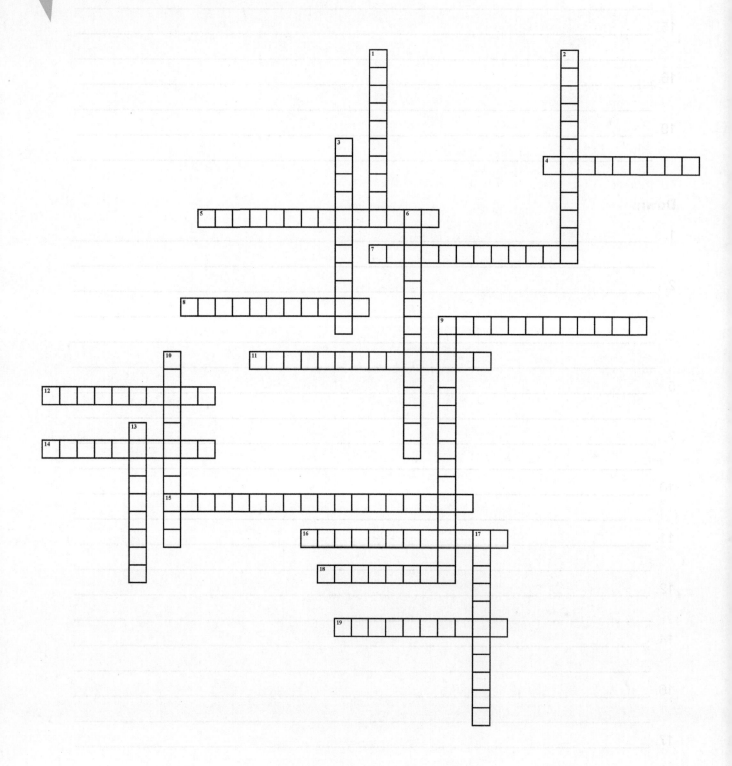

Apply critical thinking skills in a team environment   © Five Senses Education Pty Ltd and Linda Joel

Across:

4. Critical thinking skill involved with identifying the need for a new policy.

5. A person bullying others may be given one of these. (2 words)

7. All of these must be investigated when making inferences.

8. Usually made during analysis.

9. This can be affected by continual bullying and harassment.

11. An anti-bullying and harassment policy must be considered to be one of these. (2 words)

12. A critical thinking process when judgements are based on reasoning.

14. A stakeholder.

15. It is important that this is communicated when a new policy is introduced. (2 words)

16. How a lot of problems in the workplace are solved. (2 words)

18. These should not be used in a new policy as they are not always understood.

19. Access to documentation in a confidential file.

Down:

1. This is done to check if facts are correct.

2. Action taken against aggressors.

3. Part of the analysis process. (3 words)

6. When both parties have the right to be heard. (2 words)

9. Assumptions.

10. A point of view.

13. This is very important when drafting a new policy.

17. This may be offered to workers who have been bullied or harassed.

Extended response 1:

a) Outline the different critical thinking processes. (3 marks)

_____

_____

_____

_____

_____

_____

b) Explain the importance of asking questions at each stage of the critical thinking process, giving examples. (4 marks)

_____

_____

_____

_____

_____

_____

_____

_____

_____

_____

_____

c) Explain how all thinking is defined by eight elements and how each of these elements has implications for the other elements. (8 marks)

_____

_____

_____

_____

_____

_____

_____

_____

Apply critical thinking skills in a team environment

Extended response 2:

Analyse possible responses to challenges and questions from stakeholders regarding a new policy on bullying and harassment. (15 marks)

Your answer will be assessed on how well you:
- demonstrate knowledge and understanding relevant to the question
- communicate ideas and information using relevant workplace examples and industry terminology
- present a logical and cohesive response

_____

_____

_____

_____

_____

_____

_____

_____

_____

_____

_____

_____

_____

_____

_____

_____

_____

_____

_____

_____

_____

_____

_____

 © Five Senses Education Pty Ltd and Linda Joel

Apply critical thinking skills in a team environment

Chapter 4: Assessment tasks to provide evidence of ability and demonstration of knowledge of topic

Each student must provide evidence of the ability to:
- generate and present solutions to a workplace problem on at least two occasions

Each student must also be able to:
- identify and analyse workplace problems as part of a team
- develop questions on key challenges of a chosen problem
- consult relevant stakeholders to gather information on workplace problem
- use a range of creative thinking techniques as part of a team to generate ideas or responses to questions or issues
- use critical thinking processes to develop relevant questions and criteria for identified workplace issue
- present to relevant stakeholders and respond to answers
- assess feedback to identify key personal and team learnings

Each student must also demonstrate knowledge of:
- organisational and legislative frameworks
- advantages of different perspectives when asking questions
- critical thinking techniques
- applicable criteria to assess potential solutions to workplace issue
- boundaries to be considered when generating ideas and responses
- methods to develop individual critical and creative thinking skills

Instructions:

Part of these tasks are to be completed by each individual student and should be submitted on your own paper for marking. For that part that is completed in a small group, only one copy for the group needs to be submitted, but make sure that every student in the group has a copy. Submitted answers will be marked as competent or not yet competent. Any task that is deemed not yet competent must be reviewed, updated and resubmitted until it has been deemed competent.

Task 1:

Using critical thinking skills, analyse two common workplace problems of your choosing.

Instructions:

Choose one common problem encountered by workers to complete on your own and choose one common problem encountered by a business to complete in a group of two to four students. Refer to the lists of common problems experienced by workers and the business on pages 4-5 of the textbook.

For each problem:

1. Identify the problem

2. State the purpose (goal or objective) of your analysis

3. Identify the questions you would ask to gain the knowledge to solve the problem

4. Gather and present your information (facts, data, evidence), citing sources

5. Outline the concepts (theories, laws, principles, models) you have used

6. State your inferences (conclusions, solutions) and the reasons for reaching them

7. Identify any assumptions used

8. Generate implications or consequences of your conclusions

9. Identify any other points of view that could have been taken into account

Task 2:

For the common problem of your own choosing, each student must submit notes, using the following headings:

1. The organisational and legislative frameworks taken into account for this problem.

2. What questions did you ask and of whom?
   - Identify any advantages of different perspectives when asking questions.

3. Critical thinking techniques used.

4. Applicable criteria to assess potential solutions to workplace issue.

5. Boundaries that were considered when generating ideas and responses.

6. Methods used to develop individual critical and creative thinking skills.

For the common problem chosen by the group, one set of notes (with input from all students) must be submitted, using the following headings:

1. The organisational and legislative frameworks taken into account for this problem.

2. What questions did you ask and of whom?
   - Identify any advantages of different perspectives when asking questions.

3. Critical thinking techniques used.
   - Were these different when working in a group?

4. Applicable criteria to assess potential solutions to workplace issue.

5. Boundaries that were considered when generating ideas and responses.

6. Methods used to develop critical and creative thinking skills.
   - Were these different when working in a group?

Chapter 5: Suggested answers

Note: no suggested answers are given for the completed crosswords as answers will vary for each student.

Chapter 1:

1. Brainstorming takes into account suggestions from workers and consulting with others who have dealt with similar problems; evaluating all possible solutions, looking at positives and negatives; looking at the resources needed for each possible solution, including time, personnel and budget.

Marks	Criteria
2	• Detailed outline of what is involved in brainstorming possible solutions to a problem
1	• Mentions at least one point about brainstorming possible solutions to a problem

2. To monitor and evaluate the solution, you should continuously measure the progress being made and take notice of feedback from all stakeholders; make adjustments if needed; look at implementing a new plan if the first one doesn't work to expectations.

Marks	Criteria
2	• Detailed outline of how you can monitor and evaluate a solution to a problem
1	• Mentions at least one point about monitoring and evaluating a solution to a problem

3. A poor work-life balance exists when work and stress adversely affects other important aspects of a worker's life.

Marks	Criteria
2	• Detailed explanation of poor work-life balance
1	• Mentions at least one point about work-life balance

4. Other common problems include:
   - Lack of upward mobility
   - Inflexibility of schedules
   - Little recognition of contribution of workers
   - Poor leadership and low motivation of workers
   - Lack of equipment, technology and/or facilities
   - Lack of accountability often due to lack of training
   - Outdated policies and procedures as management are not keeping up-to-date

- Inadequate job descriptions so workers don't have a full understanding of their job role
- Ineffective job performance reviews which do not compare job descriptions to actual performance
- Communication is always from the top down rather than being two-way so workers do not feel valued
- Lack of suitable training so workers are often left to learn "on the job", often resulting in mistakes being made and management not being pleased with work performance

Marks	Criteria
4	• Identifies four problems
3	• Identifies three problems
2	• Identifies two problems
1	• Identifies one problem

5. Common problems encountered by the business include:

- Falling sales
- Difficult clients
- Increasing costs
- Lack of cash flow
- Ineffective marketing
- Increased competition
- Uncertainty of the future
- Damaged business reputation
- Little expansion into new markets
- Unreliable supply of raw materials
- Increasing and changing regulations
- Lack of available skilled workers for hire
- Not keeping up with technological changes

NB: explanations as to why they are a problem will vary

Marks	Criteria
4	• Identifies four problems, including an explanation why they are a problem
3	• Identifies three problems, including an explanation why they are a problem
2	• Identifies two problems, including an explanation why they are a problem
1	• Identifies one problem, with or without an explanation why they are a problem

6. Team cohesion occurs when a team remains united while working to achieve a common goal and everyone feels they have contributed to the overall success of the team.

Marks	Criteria
2	• Detailed explanation of team cohesion
1	• Mentions at least one point about team cohesion OR teams

7. Bullying and harassment can lead to a toxic workplace with low staff morale and low productivity.

Marks	Criteria
2	• Detailed explanation of the impact of bullying and harassment on a workplace
1	• Mentions at least one point about how bullying and harassment can impact on a workplace

8. Overt bullying is obvious or direct whereas covert bullying is hidden or indirect.

Marks	Criteria
2	• Good differentiation of overt and covert bullying
1	• Mentions at least one point on either overt or covert bullying.

9. The main types of bullying and harassment include:
   • Verbal: repeated hurtful remarks to make fun of someone
   • Physical: pushing, shoving, tripping and/or grabbing to intentionally hurt someone; attacking someone with a weapon like a kitchen knife
   • Psychological: continually playing mind games with someone; any comments, actions or gestures that affect someone's dignity or psychological integrity which has a lasting harmful effect
   • Sexual: unwelcome touching; making sexually explicit comments and requests that make someone feel uncomfortable; sending sexually suggestive emails or texts; asking intrusive questions, including someone's sex life; displaying pornographic material or screen savers

   Marks: 1 mark each for identifying the four types of bullying and harassment
   1 mark each for the description of the four types of bullying and harassment

10. Bullying and harassment can cause the victim to:
- Frequently change jobs
- Increase sick leave taken
- Show deterioration in work performance
- Use or misuse of alcohol and/or drugs
- Social withdraw, both at work and home
- Change the victim's normal behaviour
- Change eating habits, resulting in weight loss or gain
- Depression and other mental health conditions, with increased risk of suicide

Marks	Criteria
3	• Identifies three effects that bullying and harassment can have on the person being bullied
2	• Identifies two effects that bullying and harassment can have on the person being bullied
1	• Identifies one effect that bullying and harassment can have on the person being bullied

11. A safe working environment should provide equal opportunity for all workers, free from discrimination, harassment and bullying.

Marks	Criteria
2	• Detailed description of a safe work environment
1	• Mentions at least one point about a safe work environment

12. Behaviour that is repeatedly unreasonable, unwelcomed and unsolicited, that would be considered as being offensive, intimidating, humiliating or threatening, that can have an impact on the health and wellbeing of another worker, would be deemed as bullying or harassment.

Marks	Criteria
2	• Detailed description of behaviour that would be deemed as bullying or harassment
1	• Mentions at least one point about bullying or harassment

13. Bullying and harassment is based on a power imbalance, happens repeatedly and usually occurs to cause psychological or physical harm. This is different to a conflict which is usually a misunderstanding between two equals, and to teasing which is generally fun "give-and-take" between friends for a laugh, with no intent for harm.

Marks	Criteria
3	• Explains the difference between bullying, conflict and teasing
2	• Explains the difference between two of bullying, conflict and teasing
1	• Mentions at least one point about bullying OR teasing OR conflict

14. Bullying and harassment can also affect witnesses, everyone's families and the business itself.

Marks	Criteria
2	• Identifies at least two other people who can be affected by bullying and harassment
1	• Identifies one other person who can be affected by bullying and harassment

15. It is important to keep a diary as it is a record or evidence of what was said or done, by whom, on what day, at what time, who witnessed it and the harm it caused.

Marks	Criteria
2	• Detailed description of why it is important to keep a diary of bullying and harassment
1	• Mentions at least one point about keeping a diary about bullying and harassment

16. Data that could indicate that bullying and/or harassment is taking place include: absentee rates, incident records, exit interviews, staff turnover records and workers' compensation claims, as well as records of grievances, disputes and complaints.

Marks	Criteria
3	• Identifies three or more sources of data that could indicate that bullying and/or harassment is occurring
2	• Identifies two sources of data that could indicate that bullying and/or harassment is occurring
1	• Identifies one source of data that could indicate that bullying and/or harassment is occurring

Multiple choice and true/false:

1	2	3	4	5	6	7	8	9	10
c	b	a	c	c	a	a	b	d	c
11	**12**	**13**	**14**	**15**	**16**	**17**	**18**	**19**	**20**
d	T	F	T	T	F	T	F	F	F
21	**22**	**23**	**24**	**25**	**26**	**27**	**28**	**29**	**30**
T	T	T	T	F	T	F	T	T	F
31	**32**	**33**	**34**	**35**	**36**	**37**	**38**	**39**	**40**
T	T	F	F	T	T	F	T	T	F

Crossword:

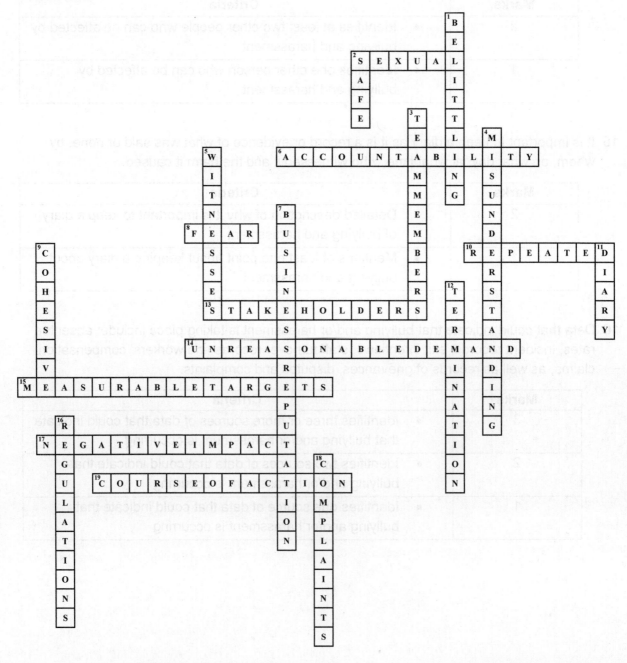

Extended response 1:

a) Answer could include: Workplace problems can be anything from a straightforward issue, like whose turn is it to clean up the kitchen, to very complicated issues, like teams not working together effectively.

Marks	Criteria
3	• Demonstrates a sound understanding of the types of problems that occur in the workplace
2	• Demonstrates some understanding of the types of problems that occur in the workplace
1	• Provides some relevant information

b) Answer could include: The steps in solving problems include:
- Identify the problem
- Define the problem
- Understand who is affected by the problem
- Brainstorm possible solutions
- Select the best course of action
- Implement the solution
- Monitor and evaluate the solution

Marks	Criteria
3	• Demonstrates a sound understanding of the steps involved in problem solving
2	• Demonstrates some understanding of the steps involved in problem solving
1	• Provides some relevant information

c) Answer could include:
- Different types of bullying and harassment: verbal, physical, psychological, sexual
- Examples of direct and indirect bullying and harassment
- Effects can include:
  - Frequent change in jobs
  - Increased sick leave being taken
  - Deterioration in work performance
  - Use or misuse of alcohol and/or drugs
  - Social withdrawal, both at work and home
  - Changes to the victim's normal behaviour
  - Changes to eating habits, resulting in weight loss or gain
  - Depression and other mental health conditions, with increased risk of suicide

Marks	Criteria
8-9	• Demonstrates an extensive knowledge of bullying and harassment and their effects on victims
6-7	• Demonstrates a thorough knowledge of bullying and harassment and their effects on victims
4-5	• Demonstrates some knowledge of bullying and harassment and their effects on victims
2-3	• Demonstrates some knowledge of bullying and harassment
1	• Provides some relevant information

Extended response 2:

Answer could include:

- Charter also known as a Workplace Discrimination, Harassment and Bullying Policy
- The procedures should set out:
  - References to current State and Federal legislation
  - Internal and external options for resolving the issue
  - Definitions of discrimination, harassment and bullying
  - The rights and responsibilities of all team members, managers and supervisors
  - Examples of each, making it clear exactly what is unacceptable in the workplace
  - To who a problem should be reported, for example your supervisor, a manager, Human Resources Dept
  - Possible outcomes, including an apology, formal warning, transfer, demotion, education or training, termination of employment

- Reasons for introducing this type of policy:
  - assist all team members in understanding their rights and responsibilities
  - to provide a safe working environment that provides equal opportunity for all workers, free from discrimination, harassment and bullying
  - to encourage diversity, which embodies sensitive and ethical appreciation and recognition of differences among all workers, encouraging inclusiveness and participation in all areas in the workplace

Marks	Criteria
13-15	• Demonstrates an extensive knowledge and understanding of bullying and harassment policies and procedures • Clearly explains the relationship between bullying and harassment policies and procedures and the amount of bullying and harassment occurring in the workplace • Communicates ideas and information using relevant workplace examples and industry terminology • Presents a logical and cohesive response
10-12	• Demonstrates a sound knowledge and understanding of bullying and harassment policies and procedures • Explains the relationship between bullying and harassment policies and procedures and the amount of bullying and harassment occurring in the workplace • Communicates using relevant workplace examples and industry terminology • Presents a logical response
7-9	• Demonstrates some knowledge and understanding of bullying and harassment policies and procedures • Shows some relationship between bullying and harassment policies and procedures and the amount of bullying and harassment occurring in the workplace • Communicates using some workplace examples and industry terminology • Demonstrates some organisation in presenting information
4-6	• Demonstrates basic knowledge and/or understanding of bullying and harassment • Uses some industry terminology
1-3	• Provides some relevant information

Chapter 2:

Short answers:

1. Critical thinking is the ability to think clearly and rationally, to be able to objectively analyse an issue or situation and the facts, data or evidence related to it, without influence from personal feelings, opinions or biases, allowing you to make logical and informed decisions.

Marks	Criteria
2	• Detailed description of critical thinking
1	• Mentions at least one point about critical thinking

2. The skills used in critical thinking include:
   - Identification of a problem and identification of the factors that influence/affect it
   - Doing research
   - Analyse and evaluate the data collected
   - Identify any bias, making sure that your own biases don't come in to it, and look at everything on an equal footing
   - Inference
   - Determining relevance
   - Curiosity
   - Drawing conclusions
   - Explanation of conclusions

Marks	Criteria
4	• Identifies seven or more critical thinking skills
3	• Identifies five or six critical thinking skills
2	• Identifies three or four critical thinking skills
1	• Identifies at one or two critical thinking skills

3. Risk assessment measures the likelihood and severity of injury associated with a problem which is important so a solution can be generated to end this problem in the workplace.

Marks	Criteria
2	• Detailed description of risk assessment
1	• Mentions at least one point about risk assessment

4. The risk matrix is a visual representation of the risk analysis. It presents the risks as a graph, rating them by category of probability and category of severity.

Marks	Criteria
2	• Detailed description of risk assessment matrix
1	• Mentions at least one point about risk assessment matrix

5. Bullying and harassment policy and procedures should include guidelines on reporting complaints, investigating complaints and consequences for those engaging in bullying and harassment behaviour.

Marks	Criteria
2	• Detailed description of guidelines that should be included in a bullying and harassment policy and procedures
1	• Mentions at least one point about bullying and harassment policy and procedures

6. Awareness raising: to raise awareness of what bullying and harassment is and when it is taking place; to explain worker responsibilities for working in a safe environment; to raise awareness of the effects of bullying and harassment can have on individuals, teams and the business itself; to outline actions that should be taken if workers believe they are being bullied or harassed

Marks	Criteria
2	• Detailed description of awareness raising
1	• Mentions at least one point about awareness raising

7. Leadership training: to enable supervisors, leaders and managers to understand the fundamentals of bullying and harassment; to learn best practice for preventing or dealing with issues as they arise; and to know their responsibilities in creating a workplace free from bullying and harassment

Marks	Criteria
2	• Detailed description of leadership training
1	• Mentions at least one point about leadership training

8. At the job level, changes can be made to:
   - Working environment, organisation of work activities, demands placed on workers, training, work hours, health and well-being standards
   - Job descriptions so person being bullied can be moved away from the aggressor
   - Physical work environment: moving furniture around, providing separate lunch areas and times

Marks	Criteria
3	• Identifies three changes that can be made at the job level
2	• Identifies two changes that can be made at the job level
1	• Identifies one change that can be made at the job level

9. Mediation is a confidential and structured process for the resolution of issues to achieve positive working relationships, that involves an independent and impartial third party who facilitates open discussions between the worker being bullied and harassed and the aggressor to diffuse situations and resolve problems of bullying and harassment

Marks	Criteria
2	• Detailed description of mediation
1	• Mentions at least one point about mediation

10. The development process usually consists of:
   - Identification of the need for a new policy
   - Consultation with all stakeholders
   - Determination of the content of the new policy
   - Draft the new policy
   - Distribution of proposed policy to all stakeholders for purpose of obtaining feedback
   - Revision of proposed policy taking into account feedback received
   - Set an implementation date
   - Communicate the new policy to all stakeholders

Marks	Criteria
3	• Detailed identification of the steps involved in developing a new policy
2	• Identifies a number of steps involved in developing a new policy
1	• Identifies at least one step involved in developing a new policy

11. Criteria are the principles or standards by which something may be judged or decided.

Marks	Criteria
2	• Detailed definition of criteria
1	• Mentions at least one point about criteria

12. Training of workers is necessary to developing a workplace culture that encourages dignity and respect. Training reduces the risk of bullying and harassment occurring because it builds worker confidence in the business's anti-bullying and harassment policy and better equips managers to understand issues and prevention strategies at the workplace level.

Marks	Criteria
2	• Detailed definition of how training reduces bullying and harassment in the workplace
1	• Mentions at least one point about training of workers

Multiple choice and true/false:

1	2	3	4	5	6	7	8	9	10
c	d	c	b	c	a	b	a	a	d
11	**12**	**13**	**14**	**15**	**16**	**17**	**18**	**19**	**20**
d	a	c	a	b	T	F	T	F	F
21	**22**	**23**	**24**	**25**	**26**	**27**	**28**	**29**	**30**
F	T	T	F	T	F	F	F	T	T
31	**32**	**33**	**34**	**35**	**36**	**37**	**38**	**39**	**40**
T	T	F	T	F	F	T	F	T	F
41	**42**	**43**	**44**	**45**					
F	T	T	T	T					

Crossword:

Down / Across answers:

1. EVIDENCE
2. PREPAREDPLAN
3. INFERENCE
4. EVALUATE
5. SUPERVISORS
6. WHOLEBUSINESS
7. COACHINGSESSS
8. IMPLEMENTCONTROLS
9. TRAINING
10. CRITERIA
11. INCONSISTENCIES
12. WORKREDEEMNS
13. CONCLUSIONS
14. REGULARLY
15. WITNESSS
16. COMMUNICATION
17. INAPPROPRIATE
18. LIKELIHOOD
19. RATIONALLY
20. REDFLAGS

Extended response 1:

1. Answer could include: At the level of the individual worker, strategies which aim to prevent and manage workplace bullying and harassment must be developed and introduced. Worker education occurs when training is provided for all workers regarding what behaviour is considered bullying and harassment (which does not include reasonable directions from management) and the effects it has in the workplace. Its' role is to teach workers how to identify that it is happening, what their responsibilities are when witnessing bullying and harassment, and how to help co-workers who are being bullied or harassed

Marks	Criteria
3	• Demonstrates a sound understanding of the role of worker education about bullying and harassment
2	• Demonstrates a some understanding of the role of worker education about bullying and harassment
1	• Provides some relevant information

2. Answer could include: The steps in a risk assessment include:
   - Considering whether workers are at risk of bullying and harassment by identifying factors that could contribute to, or encourage, this type of behaviour
   - Assessing the risk of potential harm to worker's health and safety, the likelihood of occurrence and the extent to which risks can be controlled
   - Implementing controls, depending on the risks identified
   - Monitoring and reviewing initiatives to prevent bullying and harassment to ensure that interventions are successfully carried out and any issues or difficulties implementing measures are addressed

Marks	Criteria
4	• Demonstrates a sound understanding of all four steps taken in a risk assessment
3	• Demonstrates a good understanding of the steps taken in a risk assessment
2	• Demonstrates a some understanding of the steps taken in a risk assessment
1	• Provides some relevant information

3. Answer could include:
   - Possible strategies (a range of options should be covered)
     - Business level
       - Workplace policies
       - Awareness training
       - Leadership training
       - Organisational development

- o Job level
  - Making changes to working conditions
  - Changing job descriptions
  - Changing the physical work environment
- o Individual worker level
  - Worker education
  - Coaching sessions
  - Executive coaching
  - Cognitive rehearsal
  - mediation
- Each strategy should be evaluated – a judgement should be made based on criteria or the value should be determined

Marks	Criteria
8	• Demonstrates an extensive knowledge of strategies that can eliminate bullying and harassment
6-7	• Demonstrates a thorough knowledge of strategies that can eliminate bullying and harassment
4-5	• Demonstrates some knowledge of how bullying and harassment can be eliminated
2-3	• Demonstrates some knowledge of bullying and harassment
1	• Provides some relevant information

Extended response 2:

Answer could include:

- A description of the following critical thinking skills:
  - o Identification of the problem and factors that influence it
  - o Doing research
  - o Analysing and evaluating data collected
  - o Identifying bias
  - o Inference
  - o Determining relevance
  - o Curiosity
  - o Drawing conclusions
  - o Explaining conclusions
- These skills can be used to complete a risk assessment and a risk assessment matrix (explain both)
- Explanation of a range of solutions to the problem of bullying and harassment
  - o Solutions could be implemented at the business level, the job level and the individual worker level
  - o Benefits of an integrative approach

Marks	Criteria
13-15	• Demonstrates an extensive knowledge and understanding of critical thinking skills • Clearly explains the relationship between critical thinking skills and generating solutions to bullying and harassment • Communicates ideas and information using relevant workplace examples and industry terminology • Presents a logical and cohesive response
10-12	• Demonstrates a sound knowledge and understanding of critical thinking skills • Explains the relationship between critical thinking skills and generating solutions to bullying and harassment • Communicates using relevant workplace examples and industry terminology • Presents a logical response
7-9	• Demonstrates some knowledge and understanding of critical thinking skills • Shows some link between critical thinking skills and generating solutions to bullying and harassment • Communicates using some workplace examples and industry terminology • Demonstrates some organisation in presenting information
4-6	• Demonstrates basic knowledge and/or understanding of critical thinking skills and/or generating solutions to bullying and harassment • Uses some industry terminology
1-3	• Provides some relevant information

Chapter 3:

Short answers:

1. An anti-bullying and harassment policy is often referred to as a Dignity and Respect in the Workplace Charter.

Marks	Criteria
1	• Correctly identifies the Dignity and Respect in the Workplace Charter

2. The steps involved when determining the content for a new policy include evaluating and analysing information gathered; identifying any bias; determining relevance; drawing conclusions

Marks	Criteria
2	• Detailed description of the steps involved when determining the content for a new policy
1	• Mentions at least one point about the steps involved when determining policy content

3. A policy is regarded as being a living document when it is regularly updated through discussion with all parties as the need arises.

Marks	Criteria
2	• Detailed description of a living document
1	• Mentions at least one point about a living document

4. An anti-bullying and harassment policy must be visually published and all stakeholders must know what it is, know where it is located and how to access it whenever necessary.

Marks	Criteria
2	• Detailed description of how accessible an anti-bullying and harassment should be
1	• Mentions at least one point about accessibility of an anti-bullying and harassment policy

5. Natural justice: both parties have the right to be heard, explain their perspective and to respond to other people's perspectives; additional support mechanisms should be equally made available for all parties, even if they choose to not use them; decisions must be fair and respectful and made by an impartial and unbiased person who follows all related internal procedures.

Marks	Criteria
2	• Detailed description of natural justice
1	• Mentions at least one point about natural justice

6. Successful performance in business requires fair-minded decision making, anticipation of consequences, and the evaluation of options and actions.

Marks	Criteria
2	• Detailed description of what is required for a business to succeed
1	• Mentions at least one point about business success

7. Intuitive: reactive and holistic decision-making; going with one's first instinct and reaching decisions quickly based on automatic cognitive processes such as thinking, knowing, remembering, judging and problem-solving, while making sound decisions taking in the whole situation
Reflective: procedural and rule-governed; making judgements based on reasoning, after considering options available, analysing the options using specific criteria and then drawing conclusions, taking into account procedures and rules

Marks	Criteria
4	• Detailed description of both intuitive and reflective critical thinking processes
3	• Good description of both intuitive and reflective critical thinking skills
2	• Good description of either intuitive or reflective critical thinking processes
1	• Mentions at least one relevant point

8. Questions are asked in order to fully understand the critical thinking process and give feedback along the way.

Marks	Criteria
2	• Detailed description of why questions should be asked
1	• Mentions at least one point about asking questions

9. The eight elements of thinking include:
   • Generates purposes (goals and objectives)
   • Raises questions (problems and issues)
   • Uses information (data, facts, observations and experiences)
   • Utilises concepts (ideas, theories, definitions, laws, principles and models)

- Makes inferences (conclusions and solutions)
- Makes assumptions (presuppositions and things taken for granted)
- Generates implications (consequences)
- Embodies a point of view (a frame of reference, perspective, orientation)

(1 mark for each correct answer)

10. If more than one person works on a solution to a problem, the amount of information generated, questions asked, conclusions and assumptions are going to be more comprehensive as it involves the cumulative understanding of the entire group. Discussion and debates are used to work through solutions etc which are generated by integrating everyone's ideas.

Marks	Criteria
2	• Detailed description of why more than one person should work on a solution to a problem
1	• Mentions at least one point about solving problems

Multiple choice and true/false:

1	2	3	4	5	6	7	8	9	10
b	a	b	c	d	d	a	b	T	T
11	**12**	**13**	**14**	**15**	**16**	**17**	**18**	**19**	**20**
F	F	F	F	T	T	F	F	T	T
21	**22**	**23**	**24**	**25**	**26**	**27**	**28**	**29**	**30**
F	T	F	T	T	F	T	F	F	T
31	**32**	**33**	**34**	**35**					
T	F	F	T	T					

Crossword:

1 (down) EVALUATION

2 (down) CONSEQUENCE

3 (down) PROSANDCONS

4 (across) CURIOSITY

5 (across) WRITTENWARNING

6 (down) NATURALJUSTICE

7 (across) ALTERNATIVES

8 (across) ASSUMPTIONS

9 (across) PRODUCTIVITY

9 (down) PRPSUPPOSI...

10 (down) PERSPECTIVE

11 (across) LIVINGDOCUMENT

12 (across) PROCEDURAL

13 (down) RESPECT

14 (across) MANAGEMENT

15 (across) IMPLEMENTATIONDATE

16 (across) TEAMAPPROACH

17 (down) COUNSELLING

18 (across) ACRONYMS

19 (across) RESTRICTED

RELEVANCE

Extended response 1:

a) Answer could include: Critical thinking processes can either be:

- Intuitive, reactive, and holistic decision-making: going with one's first instinct and reaching decisions quickly based on automatic cognitive processes such as thinking, knowing, remembering, judging and problem-solving, while making sound decisions taking in the whole situation

- Reflective, procedural and rule-governed: making judgements based on reasoning, after considering options available, analysing the options using specific criteria and then drawing conclusions, taking into account procedures and rules

Marks	Criteria
3	• Demonstrates a sound understanding of different critical thinking processes
2	• Demonstrates a some understanding of the critical thinking processes
1	• Provides some relevant information

b) Answer could include: When critical thinking is a collaborative team process, many questions are asked at each stage of the process. Every team member has different skills when it comes to solving problems, so they can ask each other questions to fully understand the critical thinking process and give each other feedback along the way. The questions allow all the possible solutions to be identified, that all alternatives have been considered and whether the best solution has been selected. Examples of questions asked include:

- Interpretation: how should that be interpreted?
- Analysis: what are your reasons for that decision?
- Inference: has any alternative been missed?
- Evaluation: can we trust the sources of information?
- Explanation: how was the analysis conducted?

Marks	Criteria
4	• Demonstrates a sound understanding of asking questions, including examples
3	• Demonstrates a good understanding of asking questions, including examples
2	• Demonstrates a some understanding of asking questions, with at least one example
1	• Provides some relevant information

c) Answer could include: Everyone thinks, but much of our thinking is biased, distorted, partial, uninformed or prejudiced. The success of a business depends on the quality of the thinking of individuals and teams. Whenever we think, we think for a reason. We have a point of view that is based on assumptions that lead to implications and consequences for the business. We use concepts, ideas and theories to interpret data, facts and experiences in order to answer questions, solve problems, and resolve issues. All thinking is defined by eight elements. Thinking:

- Generates purposes (goals and objectives)
- Raises questions (problems and issues)
- Uses information (data, facts, observations and experiences)
- Utilises concepts (ideas, theories, definitions, laws, principles and models)
- Makes inferences (conclusions and solutions)
- Makes assumptions (presuppositions and things taken for granted)
- Generates implications (consequences)
- Embodies a point of view (a frame of reference, perspective, orientation)

Each of these has implications for the others. For instance:

- If the purpose changes, the questions change
- If the questions change, you have to seek new information and data
- If the information is different, the concepts change
- If the concepts change, the inferences or conclusions change
- If the inferences change, you have to change your assumptions
- If the assumptions change, the implications will be different
- Different implications will result in a different point of view

Marks	Criteria
8	• Demonstrates an extensive knowledge of the elements of thinking
6-7	• Demonstrates a thorough knowledge of the elements of thinking
4-5	• Demonstrates some knowledge of the elements of thinking
2-3	• Demonstrates some knowledge of the elements of thinking
1	• Provides some relevant information

Extended response 2:

Answer may include: Many questions or challenges may arise from stakeholders concerning a new anti-bullying and harassment policy. These may concern timeframes, accessibility, confidentiality, natural justice, procedural fairness, action taken and where to get help.

Answer should cover possible responses to each of these concerns and an analysis of the relationship between them, and any implications raised.

Marks	Criteria
13-15	• Demonstrates an extensive knowledge and understanding of challenges and questions from stakeholders regarding a new policy on bullying and harassment • Clearly analyses possible responses to these challenges and questions • Communicates ideas and information using relevant workplace examples and industry terminology • Presents a logical and cohesive response
10-12	• Demonstrates a sound knowledge and understanding of challenges and questions from stakeholders regarding a new policy on bullying and harassment • Shows some analysis of possible responses to these challenges and questions • Communicates using relevant workplace examples and industry terminology • Presents a logical response
7-9	• Demonstrates some knowledge and understanding of challenges and questions from stakeholders regarding a new policy on bullying and harassment. • Explains the responses rather than analyses them • Communicates using some workplace examples and industry terminology • Demonstrates some organisation in presenting information
4-6	• Demonstrates basic knowledge and/or understanding of challenges and questions from stakeholders regarding a new policy on bullying and harassment • Uses some industry terminology
1-3	• Provides some relevant information

Chapter 4:

Note: These tasks are not awarded marks. Submitted answers will be marked as competent or not yet competent. Any task that is deemed not yet competent must be reviewed, updated and resubmitted until it has been deemed competent. Record the date when deemed competent.

Task	Competent	Not yet competent
Task 1: point 1		
Task 1: point 2		
Task 1: point 3		
Task 1: point 4		
Task 1: point 5		
Task 1: point 6		
Task 1: point 7		
Task 1: point 8		
Task 1: point 9		
Task 2: individual point 1		
Task 2: individual point 2		
Task 2: individual point 3		
Task 2: individual point 4		
Task 2: individual point 5		
Task 2: individual point 6		
Task 2: group point 1		
Task 2: group point 2		
Task 2: group point 3		
Task 2: group point 4		
Task 2: group point 5		
Task 2: group point 6		

Notes

_____

_____

_____

_____

_____

_____

_____

_____

_____

_____

_____

_____

_____

_____

_____

_____

_____

_____

_____

_____

_____

_____

_____

_____

_____

_____

_____

_____

_____